D1637217

Presented to:

_____

From:

_____

Date:

_____

TRUTH AND GRACE MEMORY BOOK

BOOK 1

Ages Two to Nine

THOMAS K. ASCOL, EDITOR

©2017 Founders Press
P.O. Box 150931
Cape Coral, FL 33915
Phone (239) 772-1400
http://www.founders.org

ISBN: 978-1-943539-05-5

Unless otherwise indicated, all Scripture quotations are from the ESV® Bible (The Holy Bible, English Standard Version®), copyright © 2001 by Crossway, a publishing ministry of Good News Publishers. Used by permission. All rights reserved.

A Catechism for Boys and Girls is reprinted with adaptation with permission from Carey Publications Ltd., 75 Woodhill Road, Leeds LS16 7BZ, United Kingdom.

Cover Design by Joshua Noom

TABLE OF
CONTENTS

"

He established a testimony in Jacob

and appointed a law in Israel,

which he commanded our fathers

to teach to their children,

that the next generation might know them,

the children yet unborn,

and arise and tell them to their children,

so that they should set their hope in God

and not forget the works of God,

but keep his commandments.

"

PSALMS 78:5-7

To
Donna,
our children,
our grandchildren,
and children yet unborn

"

Give your children big truths they can grow
into rather than light explanations they will
grow out of.

"

TEDD TRIPP

"

I learned more about Christianity from my
mother than from all the theologians in England.

"

JOHN WESLEY

INTRODUCTION

Dr. Thomas K. Ascol

Psalm 78 casts a multi-generational vision for the people of God. Asaph declares his intention to pass on to his children that which he and his generation learned from their fathers. By doing so, his children, in turn, can teach their children. "He established a testimony in Jacob and appointed a law in Israel, which he commanded our fathers to teach to their children, that the next generation might know them, the children yet unborn, and arise and tell them to their children" (Psalm 78:5-6).

The Bible teaches that children are "a heritage from the Lord" and that "the fruit of the womb is His reward" (Psalm 127:3). Each child is a gift from God. This makes parents stewards of God, entrusted with one (or more) of His greatest blessings. It also means that those who work with children are involved in a high calling.

The Truth and Grace Memory Books (*TAG* books) are designed to help parents, churches and children's workers as they fulfill that calling. Three primary ingredients are found in each book.

First and foremost is the Word of God. Several passages have been carefully selected for memorization. All Scripture throughout the Scripture Memory section is in the English Standard Version. Key Bible verses as well as longer portions are designed to introduce children to the overall scope and purpose of God's creative, providential and redemptive activity. The student who completes all three books will memorize (among other texts) the Ten Commandments, the Beatitudes, the Lord's prayer, 1 Corinthians 13, various Psalms (including 119!), plus all the books of the Bible.

Why place such an emphasis on memorizing Scripture? Listen to the Psalmist's answer: "I have stored up your word in my heart that I might not sin against You" (Psalm 119:11). Furthermore, consider the great promise God makes in Isaiah 55:10–11: "For as the rain and the snow come down from heaven, and do not return there but water the earth, making it bring forth and sprout, giving seed to the sower and bread to the eater, so shall my word be that goes out from my mouth; it shall not return to me empty, but it shall accomplish that which I purpose, and shall succeed in the thing for which I sent it." God's Spirit uses the Scripture to speak to adults and children of all ages, calling them to faith in Christ and directing in the paths of real discipleship. Therefore, as a parent who prays for the salvation and spiritual growth of your child, you must be diligent in teaching him or her the Word of God.

A second element in the workbook is a selection of sound Christian hymns to be learned and memorized. Many of these are familiar (such as the Doxology) and can be learned by very small children. Others are not so well-known but are profound in their communication of biblical truth. In all, more than 2 dozen great hymns of the faith are included.

A WORD ABOUT CATECHISMS

The third, and perhaps least familiar, ingredient are catechisms. A good catechism is a very effective tool in the hands of a dedicated parent or teacher. Each *TAG* book is built around a trustworthy, Baptist catechism. That term —"Baptist catechism"—may sound strange to many modern Baptists. They may think, as I did early in my life, that "catechism" is a Roman Catholic, Lutheran or, at best, Presbyterian word.

Of course, that simply is not true. "Catechize" is anglicized version of the Greek word, *katekeo*, which simply means "to teach." It appears, in various forms, several times in the Greek New Testament (it is translated as "taught" in Luke 1:4 and Acts 18:25).

Anyone, then, who has been taught has in some sense been catechized. But the word came to refer to a specific type of instruction early in church history. New Christians were taught the essentials of the faith by learning how to answer specific questions, which were eventually grouped together and came to be referred to simply as a "catechism."

Tom Nettles has called the 16th-century Protestant Reformation the "golden age" of catechisms. In 1562 what is arguably the most influential one of all was published as the Heidelberg Catechism. Leading reformers, most notably Martin Luther and John Calvin, produced catechisms to teach both the essentials and distinctives of their faith. In the next century, the first modern Baptists followed suit.

Early Baptist leaders regarded catechetical instruction as a valuable method to teach both children and adults the doctrinal content of the Bible. Keach's Catechism (whose author, Benjamin Keach—a 17th-century English Baptist—modeled it after the Shorter Catechism of the Westminster Assembly) was widely used among Baptists in both England and America. Charles Spurgeon (19th-century English Baptist leader) revised it slightly and reissued it for use in the Metropolitan Tabernacle.

Early Southern Baptists freely employed catechisms. One of the first publications which the Sunday School Board produced was a catechism by James Boyce, founder and first President of Southern Seminary. John Broadus also wrote a catechism which was published by the board in the 19th century. Lottie Moon used a catechism in her missionary work in China.

The *TAG* Books stand firmly in this stream of Orthodox, Protestant and Baptist catechetical instruction. Each of the three books is based on a specific catechism. *The Baptist Catechism* is reproduced in the second book, and we use this original version of the catechism so that it matches *The Baptist Catechism* set to music (which can be purchased from Founders Ministries). A simpler, more elementary one, *A Catechism for Boys and Girls*, is used in the first and *The Heidelberg Catechism for Baptists* (which draws on *The Orthodox Catechism* of 1680) is used in the third.

A WORD TO PARENTS

Raising children in the 21st century is challenging, to say the least. The temptation on parents to merely get by is great. Sometimes moms and dads simply want to make it through with the fewest possible conflicts. When this attitude is adopted parents become passive and children learn to be manipulative and the result is that neither parents nor children are happy. Though tragic, it is sadly not uncommon to see Christian homes where parents have defaulted on the responsibilities that God has entrusted to them.

Teaching their children the Word of God is at the forefront of responsibilities for Christian parents. God specifically calls Christian parents to raise their children "in the discipline and instruction of the Lord" (Ephesians 6:4). You cannot be passive and fulfill this responsibility to "bring them up" in the proper way. Prayer, discipline, godly example, and consistent, continuous, clear instruction are required.

The comprehensive nature of this responsibility is spelled out in Deuteronomy 6:4–6.

"Hear, O Israel: The LORD our God, the LORD is one. You shall love the LORD your God with all your heart and with all your soul and with all your might. And these words that I command you today shall be on your heart. You shall teach them diligently to your children, and shall talk of them when you sit in your house, and when you walk by the way, and when you lie down, and when you rise."

In the face of such a daunting responsibility I cannot overstate the value of a well-constructed catechism to help parents in this work. By learning such a catechism a child (or adult for that matter) will be introduced to the overall biblical scheme of salvation. Such discipline will frame the mind for receiving and understanding every part of the Bible. A good catechism trains a person to read the Bible theologically.

God places the responsibility for raising children squarely on the shoulders of their parents. It is not primarily the job of church leaders or the pastor. If you are a parent then recognizing and accepting this responsibility is one of the most important things you can do. If you do not invest your time and effort to teach your children about God, be assured someone else will. Your children will be discipled by someone. They may get their ideas about God primarily from television, music or social media. If so, then they are likely to be taught that God, if He exists at all, is an irrelevant, indulgent being that is little more than a nice, kindly old man. If you do not teach your children truth and righteousness, be assured that there are a multitude of teachers in this world who would deceive them into thinking that truth is personal and morality is relative.

As a pastor I have spent my life teaching the church I serve to believe sound doctrine and to stand against the false teachers of our age whose views would destroy the souls of our young people. As a Christian you have every right to expect that the sermons and teaching heard in your church will reinforce the godly principles which you are trying to teach at home. But you have no right to expect your church to take the place of the home. God has given to parents the responsibility of teaching their children divine truth.

The *TAG* books have been designed to help you fulfill that assignment. The emphasis is on memorization. Some modern educators question the wisdom of teaching young children to memorize. Concern usually centers on the fear that the child is merely committing to memory meaningless words. This is a real danger—that we will be satisfied with hearing our children merely recite back to us words and sentences of which they have no understanding. That is why parents should carefully teach their children the material in these books. Personal understanding should always be the goal of our teaching. But understanding grows over time (mine has; hasn't yours?). Truth committed to memory provides the building blocks for such growth.

I originally produced the *TAG* books in the late 1990s for the parents and children in Grace Baptist Church of Cape Coral, Florida. I borrowed from and leaned on the work of many people, including Paul Settle, Fred Malone, Bill Ascol, Karen Leach, Judy Veilleux and, of course, my wife, Donna. Founders Press first published the *TAG* books in 2000 and then again in 2005. For this new edition I owe a debt of gratitude to Jared and Heather Longshore, whose determination, thoughtfulness and creativity have made this work more accessible to a new generation of parents and children. It is a testimony to God's grace in reviving the work of His gospel that they continue to find a wide readership. My prayer has been and remains that the Lord will use these books to help parents raise generations of men and women who are mighty in His Word and Spirit and who will take the wonderful news of Jesus Christ to the remaining hard places in our world.

Donna and I loved catechizing our children. Now we love watching our children who have become parents catechizing our grandchildren. It is to those children, their spouses and our grandchildren that the Truth and Grace Memory Books are dedicated.

HOW TO USE THIS MEMORY BOOK

I remember how intimidated I was when Donna and I made our first attempts to start catechizing our firstborn. After many starts and stops and lots of mistakes, we finally settled into a healthy rhythm of incorporating questions from the catechism both in set times and informal times with her and her siblings. Following are some of the lessons we learned along the way.

Discuss the material being memorized with your child. This should be done during the actual memorization as well as at other opportune times in the day. Daily experiences and observations provide a world of opportunities to illustrate and apply God's Word. For example, those pesky night frights that young children occasionally have become wonderful occasions to comfortingly remind them that, though we cannot see God, He always sees us.

Take time to define difficult terms. Question your child in order to discover the level of his understanding. When you feel that understanding is being achieved, pray with and for the child, including in your prayer some of the concepts just discussed. Expect your children to learn, and rejoice with them over their growth in knowledge and understanding of God's Word.

No matter what the age of your children, if you will begin immediately, and continue consistently, to teach them with this workbook, you will instill in them a comprehensive awareness of the Bible's whole system of revealed truth. Obviously, the earlier a child begins, the better. But these books have been designed to be useful to young people as well to children and preschoolers.

Following are some specific suggestions that come from my experience.

1. Make this workbook something very special in your child's life. Emphasize the importance of learning God's Word. If you are genuinely excited about it, most likely your children will be also.

2. Incorporate it into your regular time of family prayer and devotion. After you have read a portion of God's Word, or some Bible story book, and have prayed, take a few minutes to work on a specific verse or question. Learn to sing the hymns together as a family. You can do it! You simply have to make the effort.

3. Encourage precise memorization. If they are going to spend the time and effort to learn it, they might as well learn it accurately.

4. Be very positive. Try not to let the workbook become a battleground where a contest of the wills (child's vs. parent's) occurs. This does not mean that you let the child dictate when he will or will not work on the material. Rather, do not let yourself get into the position where you are violating biblical principles (by employing

rage, sarcasm, ridicule, empty threats, etc.) in your zeal to have your child learn the Bible! Instead, make it an enjoyable—and at times, even fun—time. Donna and I would often let our children ask us the questions.

5. Date and sign each step. At the back of the workbook there are places for the parent to signify that the student has completed the assignments. Treat each one as a significant milestone and encourage your child to keep progressing.

6. Go at your child's own rate. Children, like adults, learn differently and at different tempos. The workbook is designed so that the material can be covered as quickly or slowly as needed. Do not hesitate to move beyond the stated age levels. Remember, these are merely suggestions.

7. Discuss the content of the verses, catechism questions or hymns being learned. Help your child understand what they are saying. Remember, the goal is spiritual understanding, not mechanical regurgitation.

8. Review. Avoid placing such an emphasis on advancement that your child is tempted to utilize only his or her short-term rather than long-term memory.

9. Rejoice. Your child is learning Bible truths which some adults will never know. Thank the Lord for the privilege of teaching your children about Him. Be encouraged as you hear them reciting the Word of God and expressing important biblical truths.

10. Pray. Ask God to drive His Word deep into the heart and conscience of each child. Pray that He will send His Spirit to teach them inwardly the truth about sin and judgment, heaven and hell, Jesus and salvation. As you diligently teach your children, labor in prayer for them until you see Christ being formed in them.

11. Encourage other parents. We all need it. Make a conscious effort to give it. Training our children in the way of the Lord is a high calling. We are constantly tempted to neglect it. We all fail at some point and at some time. Resolve to be an encourager.

"

Believe me... the church of God will never be preserved without catechesis.

"

JOHN CALVIN

A CATECHISM FOR BOYS AND GIRLS

1. Who made you?
    God made me.
    (Genesis 1:26, 27; 2:7; Ecclesiastes 12:1; Acts 17:24–29)

2. What else did God make?
    God made all things.
    (Genesis 1, esp. vv. 1, 31; Acts 14:15; Romans 11:36; Colossians 1:16)

3. Why did God make you and all things?
    For His own glory.
    (Psalm 19: 1; Jeremiah 9:23, 24; Revelation 4:11; 5:13)

4. How can you glorify God?
By loving Him and doing what He commands.
(Ecclesiastes 12:13; Mark 12:29–31; John
15:8–10; 1 Corinthians 10:31)

5. Why ought you to glorify God?
Because He made me and takes care of me.
(Romans 11:36; Revelation 4:11; cf. Daniel
5:23)

6. Are there more gods than one?
There is only one God.
(Deuteronomy 6:4; Jeremiah 10:10; Mark
12:29; Acts 17:22–31)

7. In how many persons does this one God exist?
In three persons.
(Matthew 3:16, 17; John 5:23; 10:30; 14:9, 10;
15:26; 16:13 –15; 1 John 5:20, 2 John 9;
Revelation 1:4, 5)

8. Who are they?
The Father, the Son and the Holy Spirit.
(Matthew 28:19; 2 Corinthians 13:14; 1 Peter
1:2; Jude 20, 21)

9. Who is God?
God is a Spirit, and does not have a body like men.
(John 4:24; 2 Corinthians 3:17; 1 Timothy
1:17)

10. Where is God?
    God is everywhere.
    (Psalm 139:7 –12; Jeremiah 23:23, 24; Acts
    17:27, 28)

11. Can you see God?
    No. I cannot see God, but He always sees me.
    (Exodus 33:20; John 1: 18; 1 Timothy 6:16;
    Psalm 139, esp. vv. 1–5: Proverbs 5:21;
    Hebrews 4:12, 13)

12. Does God know all things?
    Yes. Nothing can be hidden from God.
    (1 Chronicles 28:9; 2 Chronicles 16:9; Luke
    12:6, 7; Romans 2:16)

13. Can God do all things?
    Yes. God can do all His holy will.
    (Psalm 147:5; Jeremiah 32:17; Daniel 4:34,
    35; Ephesians 1: 11)

14. Where do you learn how to love and obey God?
    In the Bible alone.
    (Job 11:7; Psalm 119:104; Isaiah 8:20;
    Matthew 22:29; 2 Timothy 3:15–17)

15. Who wrote the Bible?
    Holy men who were taught by the Holy Spirit.
    (1 Peter 1:20, 21; Acts 1: 16; 2 Timothy 3:16; 1
    Peter 1:10, 11)

16. Who were our first parents?
Adam and Eve.
(Genesis 2:18–25; 3:20; 5:1, 2; Acts 17:26; 1
Timothy 2:13)

17. Of what were our first parents made?
God made the body of Adam out of the ground,
and formed Eve from the body of Adam.
(Genesis 2:7; 21–23; 3:19; Psalm 103:14)

18. What did God give Adam and Eve besides bodies?
He gave them souls that could never die.
(1 Corinthians 15:45: Ecclesiastes 12:7;
Zechariah 12:1)

19. Have you a soul as well as a body?
Yes. I have a soul that can never die.
(Matthew 10:28; Mark 8:34–38; 12:30)

20. How do you know that you have a soul?
Because the Bible tells me so.
(Matthew 10:28; Mark 8:34–38; 12:30)

21. In what condition did God make Adam and Eve?
He made them holy and happy.
(Genesis 1:26–28; Psalm 8:4–8)

22. Did Adam and Eve stay holy and happy?
No. They sinned against God.
(Genesis 3:1–7; Ecclesiastes 7:29; Hosea 6:7
where "men" = Adam)

23. What is sin?
Sin is any transgression of the law of God.
(1 John 3:4; Romans 3:20; James 2:9–11)

24. What is meant by transgression?
Doing what God forbids.
(1 Samuel 13:8–14; 15:22, 23; Hosea 6:7;
Romans 1:21–32)

25. What was the sin of our first parents?
Eating the forbidden fruit.
(Genesis 2:16, 17; 3:6)

26. Why did they eat the forbidden fruit?
Because they did not believe what God had said.
(Genesis 3:1–6; cf. Hebrews 11:6)

27. Who tempted them to this sin?
The devil tempted Eve, and she gave the fruit
to Adam.
(Genesis 3:1–13; 2 Corinthians 11:3; 1
Timothy 2:13,14; cf. Revelation 12:9)

28. What happened to our first parents when
they had sinned?
Instead of being holy and happy, they
became sinful and miserable.
(Genesis 3:14 –24; 4:1–24; James 1:14, 15)

29. What effect did the sin of Adam have on all
     mankind?
     All mankind is born in a state of sin and
     misery.
     (Psalm 51:5; Romans 5:12, 18, 19; 1
     Corinthians 15:21, 22; 1 John 5:19)

30. What do we inherit from Adam as a result of
     this original sin?
     A sinful nature.
     (1 Kings 8:46; Psalm 14:2, 3; 58:3;
     Ecclesiastes 9:3; Matthew 15:18–20; John
     2:24, 25; Romans 8:7)

31. What does every sin deserve?
     The anger and judgment of God.
     (Deuteronomy 27:26; Romans 1:18; 2:2;
     Galatians 3:10; Ephesians 5:6)

32. Can anyone go to heaven with this sinful
     nature?
     No. Our hearts must be changed before we
     can be fit for heaven.
     (Jeremiah 31:33, 34; Ezekiel 36:25–27; John
     1:12, 13; 3:1–10; 1 John 5:1, 4, 18)

33. What is a change of heart called?
     Regeneration.
     (Titus 3:5–6)

34. Who can change a sinner's heart?
    The Holy Spirit alone.
    (John 3:3; Romans 8:6–11; 1 Corinthians 2:9–
    14; 2 Thessalonians 2:13, 14; Titus 3:5–6)

35. What is righteousness?
    It is God's goodness.
    (Exodus 33:19; 34:6; Psalm 33:5; Hosea 3:5;
    Romans 11:22)

36. Can anyone be saved by his own righteousness?
    No. No one is good enough for God.
    (Proverbs 20:9; Ecclesiastes 7:20; Romans
    3:10–23)

37. What is a covenant?
    An agreement between two or more persons.
    (1 Samuel 18:3; Matthew 26:14, 15)

38. What is the covenant of grace?
    The agreement God made with His elect
    people to save them from their sins.
    (Genesis 17:1–8; Romans 11:27; Hebrews
    10:16, 17)

39. What did Christ undertake in the covenant
    of grace?
    To keep the whole law for His people and to
    suffer the punishment due to their sins.
    (Romans 8:3, 4; Galatians 4:4, 5; Hebrews
    9:14, 15)

40. Did our Lord Jesus Christ ever sin?
No. He was holy, blameless and undefiled.
(Hebrews 7:26; Luke 23:47; Hebrews 4:15; 1
Peter 2:22; 1 John 3:5)

41. How could the Son of God suffer?
Christ, the Son of God, took flesh and blood,
that He might obey and suffer as a man.
(John 1:14; Romans 8:3; Galatians 4:4;
Philippians 2:7, 8; Hebrews 2:14, 17; 4:15)

42. What is meant by the atonement?
Christ satisfying divine justice, by His
sufferings and death, in the place of sinners.
(Mark 10:45; Acts 13:38, 39; Romans 3:24–
26; 5:8, 9; 2 Corinthians 5:19–21; Galatians
3:13; 1 Peter 3:18)

43. What did God the Father undertake in the
covenant of grace?
To justify, adopt and sanctify those for whom
Christ should die.
(Romans 8:29–33; Hebrews 10:9, 10; 1
Corinthians 1:8, 9; Philippians 1:6; 1
Thessalonians 4:3, 7)

44. What is justification?
It is God regarding sinners as if they had
never sinned and granting them
righteousness.
(Zechariah 3:1–5; Romans 3:24–26; 4:5; 8:33;
2 Corinthians 5:21; Hebrews 8:12)

45. What is sanctification?
It is God making sinners holy in heart and conduct.
(John 17:17; Ephesians 2:10; 4:22–24; Philippians 2:12–13; 1 Thessalonians 5:23)

46. For whom did Christ obey and suffer?
For those whom the Father had given Him.
(Isaiah 53:8; Matthew 1:21; John 10:11, 15, 16, 26–29; 17:9; Hebrews 2:13)

47. What kind of life did Christ live on earth?
A life of perfect obedience to the law of God.
(Matthew 5:17; Romans 10:4; 1 Peter 2:21, 22)

48. What kind of death did Christ die?
The painful and shameful death of the cross.
(Psalm 22; Isaiah 53; the Gospel records)

49. Who will be saved?
Only those who repent of sin and believe in Christ.
(Mark 1:15; Luke 13:3,5; Acts 2:37–41; 16:30, 31; 20:21; 26:20)

50. What is it to repent?
To be sorry for sin, and to hate and forsake it because it is displeasing to God.
(Luke 19:8–10; Romans 6:1, 2; 2 Corinthians 7:9–11; 1 Thessalonians 1:9, 10)

51. What is it to believe in Christ?
    To trust in Christ alone for salvation.
    (John 14:6; Acts 4:12; 1 Timothy 2:5; 1 John
    5:11, 12)

52. Can you repent and believe in Christ by your
    own power?
    No. I can do nothing good without God's
    Holy Spirit.
    (John 3:5, 6; 6:44; Romans 8:2, 5, 8–11; 1
    Corinthians 2:9–14; Galatians 5:17, 18;
    Ephesians 2:4–6)

53. How can you receive the Holy Spirit?
    God has told us that we must pray to Him for
    the Holy Spirit.
    (Luke 11:9–13; John 4:10; 16:24)

54. How were godly persons saved before the
    coming of Christ?
    By believing in the Savior to come.
    (John 8:56; Galatians 3:8, 9; 1 Corinthians
    10:1–4; Hebrews 9:15; 11:13)

55. How did they show their faith?
    By offering sacrifices on God's altar.
    (Exodus 24:3–8; 1 Chronicles 29:20–25;
    Hebrews 9:19–23; 10:1; 11:28)

56. What did these sacrifices represent?
Christ, the Lamb of God, who was to die for sinners.
(Exodus 12:46; cf. John 19:36; Hebrews 9 & 10; John 1:29; 1 Corinthians 5:7; 1 Peter 1:19)

57. What does Christ do for His people?
He does the work of a prophet, a priest and a king.
(Matthew 13:57; John 18:37; Hebrews 1:1–3; 5:5–10; Revelation 1:5)

58. Why is Christ a prophet?
Because He teaches us the will of God.
(Deuteronomy 18:15, 18; John 1:18; 4:25; 14:23, 24; 1 John 5:20)

59. Why is Christ a priest?
Because He died for our sins and prays to God for us.
(Psalm 110:4; 1 Timothy 2:5, 6; Hebrews 4:14–16; 7:24, 25; 1 John 2:1, 2)

60. Why is Christ a king?
Because He rules over us and defends us.
(Psalm 2:6–9; Matthew 28:18–20; Ephesians 1:19–23; Colossians 1:13, 18; Revelation 15:3, 4)

61. Why do you need Christ as a prophet?
Because I am ignorant.
(Job 11:7; Matthew 11:25–27; John 6:67, 69; 17:25, 26; 1 Corinthians 2:14–16; 2 Corinthians 4:3–6)

62. Why do you need Christ as a priest?
    Because I am guilty.
    (Proverbs 20:9; Ecclesiastes 7:20; Romans
    3:19–23; Hebrews 10:14, 27, 28; 1 John 1:8, 9)

63. Why do you need Christ as a king?
    Because I am weak and helpless.
    (John 15:4, 5; 2 Corinthians 12:9; Philippians
    4:13; Colossians 1:11; Jude 24, 25)

64. How many commandments did God give on
    Mount Sinai?
    Ten Commandments.
    (Exodus 20:1–17; Deuteronomy 5:1–22)

65. What are the Ten Commandments
    sometimes called?
    God's moral law.
    (Luke 20:25–28; Romans 2:14,15; 10:5)

66. What do the first four commandments
    teach?
    Our duty to God.
    (Deuteronomy 6:5, 6; 10:12, 13)

67. What do the last six commandments teach?
    Our duty to our fellow men.
    (Deuteronomy 10:19; Micah 6:8; cf. Galatians
    6:10)

68. What is the sum of the Ten
    Commandments?
    To love God with all my heart, and my
    neighbor as myself.
    (Deuteronomy 6:1–15; 11:1; Matthew 22:35–
    40; James 2:8)

69. Who is your neighbor?
    All my fellow men are my neighbors.
    (Luke 10:25–37; 6:35)

70. Is God pleased with those who love and obey
    Him?
    Yes. He says, "I love them that love Me."
    (Pr.8:17; Exodus 20:6)

71. Is God pleased with those who do not love
    and obey Him?
    No. "God is angry with the wicked every
    day."
    (Psalm 7:11; Malachi 2:17; Proverbs 6:16–19)

72. What is the first commandment?
    The first commandment is, "You shall have
    no other gods before Me."
    (Exodus 20:3; Deuteronomy 5:7)

73. What does the first commandment teach us?
    To worship God only.
    (Isaiah 45:5, 6; Matthew 4:10; Revelation
    22:8, 9)

74. What is the second commandment?
The second commandment is, "You shall not make for yourself any carved image, or any likeness of anything that is in heaven above, or that is in the earth beneath, or that is in the water under the earth: you shall not bow down to them nor serve them. For I, the LORD your God, am a jealous God, visiting the iniquity of the fathers on the children to the third and fourth generations of those that hate Me, but showing mercy to thousands, to those who love Me, and keep My commandments."
(Exodus 20:4–6; Deuteronomy 5:8–10)

75. What does the second commandment teach us?
To worship God in the right way and to avoid idolatry.
(Isaiah 44:9–20; 46:5–9; John 4:23, 24; Acts 17:29)

76. What is the third commandment?
The third commandment is, "You shall not take the name of the LORD your God in vain; for the LORD will not hold him guiltless who takes His name in vain."
(Exodus 20:7; Deuteronomy 5:11)

77. What does the third commandment teach us?
To reverence God's name, word and works.
(Isaiah 8:13; Psalm 29:2; 138:2; Revelation 15:3, 4)

78. What is the fourth commandment?
The fourth commandment is, "Remember
the Sabbath day to keep it holy. Six days you
shall labor and do all your work, but the
seventh day is the Sabbath of the LORD your
God. In it you shall do no work: you nor your
son, nor your daughter, nor your
manservant, nor your maidservant, nor your
cattle, nor your stranger who is within your
gates. For in six days the LORD made
heaven and earth, the sea, and all that is in
them, and rested the seventh day. Therefore
the LORD blessed the Sabbath day, and
hallowed it."
(Exodus 20:811; 23:12; Deuteronomy 5:12–15)

79. What does the fourth commandment teach us?
To keep the Sabbath holy.
(Leviticus 19:20; 23:3; Isaiah 58:13, 14)

80. What day of the week is the Christian Sabbath?
The first day of the week, called the Lord's Day.
(Acts 20:7; Revelation 1:10)

81. Why is it called the Lord's Day?
Because on that day Christ rose from the dead.
(Matthew 28:1; Mk 16:9; Luke 24:1–6; John
20:1)

82.   How should the Sabbath be kept?
      In prayer and praise, in hearing and reading
      God's Word, and in doing good to our fellow men.
      (Isaiah 58:13, 14; Matthew 12:10–13; Luke
      4:16; Acts 20:7; 1 Corinthians 16:2)

83.   What is the fifth commandment?
      The fifth commandment is, "Honor your
      father and your mother, that your days may
      be long upon the land which the LORD your
      God is giving you."
      (Exodus 20:12; Deuteronomy 5:16)

84.   What does the fifth commandment teach us?
      To love and obey our parents.
      (Matthew 15:3–6; Ephesians 6:1–3;
      Colossians 3:20)

85.   What is the sixth commandment?
      The sixth commandment is, "You shall not
      murder."
      (Exodus 20:13; Deuteronomy 5:17)

86.   What does the sixth commandment teach us?
      To avoid hatred.
      (Matthew 5:21–24; 1 John 3:15)

87.   What is the seventh commandment?
      The seventh commandment is, "You shall
      not commit adultery."
      (Exodus 20:14; Deuteronomy 5:18)

88.   What does the seventh commandment teach us?
      To be pure in heart, language and conduct.
      (Matthew 5:27, 28; Ephesians 5:3–5;
      Philippians 4:8, 9)

89.   What is the eighth commandment?
      The eighth commandment is, "You shall not steal."
      (Exodus 20:15; Deuteronomy 5:19)

90.   What does the eighth commandment teach us?
      To be honest and not to take the things of others.
      (Exodus 23:4; Proverbs 21:6, 7; Ephesians 4:28)

91.   What is the ninth commandment?
      The ninth commandment is, "You shall not bear false witness against your neighbor."
      (Exodus 20:16; Deuteronomy 5:20)

92.   What does the ninth commandment teach us?
      To tell the truth and not to speak evil of others.
      (Psalm 15:13; Zechariah 8:16; 1 Corinthians 13:6; James 4:11)

93. What is the tenth commandment?
The tenth commandment is, "You shall not covet your neighbor's house, you shall not covet your neighbor's wife, nor his manservant, nor his maidservant, nor his ox, nor his donkey, nor any thing that is your neighbor's."
(Exodus 20:17; Deuteronomy 5:21; Romans 7:7)

94. What does the tenth commandment teach us?
To be content with what we have.
(Philippians 4:1 1; 1 Timothy 6:6–8; Hebrews 13:5)

95. Can any man keep these Ten Commandments perfectly?
No mere man, since the fall of Adam, ever did or can keep the Ten Commandments perfectly.
(Proverbs 20:9; Ecclesiastes 7:20; Romans 3:19, 20; James 2:10; 1 John 1:8, 10)

96. Of what use are the Ten Commandments to us?
They teach us our duty and show us our need of a Savior.
(I Timothy 1:8–11; Romans 3:20; Galatians 3:24)

97. What is prayer?
Prayer is talking with God.
(Genesis 17:22; 18:33; Nehemiah 1:4–11; 2:4; Matthew 6:6; Romans 8:26, 27)

98. In whose name should we pray?
Only in the name of Christ.
(John 14:13, 14; 16:23, 24; Hebrews 4:14–16)

99. What has Christ given to teach us how to pray?
The Lord's Prayer.
(Matthew 6:5–15; Luke 11:1–13)

100. Repeat the Lord's Prayer.
"Our Father in heaven, hallowed be Your name. Your kingdom come. Your will be done on earth, as it is in heaven. Give us this day our daily bread. And forgive us our debts as we forgive our debtors. And lead do not lead us into temptation, but deliver us from the evil one. For Yours is the kingdom and the power and the glory forever. Amen."

101. How many petitions are there in the Lord's Prayer?
Six.

102. What is the first petition?
"Hallowed be Your name."
(Matthew 6:9; Luke 11:2)

103. What do we pray for in the first petition?
That God's name may be honored by us and all men.
(Psalm 8:1; 72:17–19; 113:1–3; 145:21; Isaiah 8:13)

104. What is the second petition?
"Thy kingdom come."
(Matthew 6:10; Luke 11:2)

105. What do we pray for in the second petition?
That the gospel may be preached in all the
world, and believed and obeyed by us and
all men.
(Matthew 28:19, 20; John 17:20, 21; Acts 8:12;
28:30, 31; 2 Thessalonians 3:1)

106. What is the third petition?
"Your will be done on earth as it is in
heaven."
(Matthew 6:10; Luke 11:2)

107. What do we pray for in the third petition?
That men on earth may serve God as the
angels do in heaven.
(Psalm 67; 103:19–22; John 9:31; Revelation
4:11)

108. What is the fourth petition?
"Give us this day our daily bread."
(Matthew 6:11; Luke 11:3)

109. What do we pray for in the fourth petition?
That God will give us all things needful for
our bodies.
(Psalm 145:15, 16; Proverbs 30:8, 9; 1
Timothy 4:4, 5)

110. What is the fifth petition?
"And forgive us our debts, as we forgive our debtors."
(Matthew 6:12; Luke 11:4)

111. What do we pray for in the fifth petition?
That God will pardon our sins and help us to forgive those who have sinned against us.
(Psalm 51: Matthew 5:23, 24; 18:21–35; 1 John 4:20, 21)

112. What is the sixth petition?
"And do not lead us into temptation, but deliver us from the evil one."
(Matthew 6:13; Luke 11:4)

113. What do we pray for in the sixth petition?
That God will keep us from sin.
(1 Chronicles 4:10; Psalm 119:11; Matthew 26:41)

114. How does the Holy Spirit bring us to salvation?
He uses the Bible, which is the Word of God.
(1 Thessalonians 1:5, 6; 2:13; 2 Timothy 3:15, 16; James 1:18; 1 Peter 1:22, 23)

115. How can we know the Word of God?
We are commanded to hear, read and search the Scriptures.
(Matthew 21:42; 22:29; 2 Timothy 3:14–17; 1 Peter 2:2; Revelation 3:22)

116. What is a church?
An assembly of baptized believers met together under the preaching of the Word of God.
(Matthew 18:20; Acts 2:42)

117. What two ordinances did Christ give to His Church?
Baptism and the Lord's Supper.
(Matthew 28:19; 1 Corinthians 11:24–26)

118. Why Did Christ give these ordinances?
To show that His disciples belong to Him, and to remind them of what He has done for them.
(Matthew 28:19; 1 Corinthians 11:24–26)

119. What is baptism?
The dipping of believers into water, as a sign of their union with Christ in His death, burial and resurrection.
(John 3:23; Acts 2:41; 8:12, 35–38; Colossians 2:12)

120. What is the purpose of baptism?
To show believers that God has cleansed them from their sins through Jesus Christ.
(Acts 22:16; Colossians 2:11–14)

121. Who are to be baptized?
Only those who repent of their sins and believe in Christ for salvation.
(Acts 2:37–41; 8:12; 18:8; 19:4, 5)

122. Should babies be baptized?
No; because the Bible neither commands it,
nor gives any example of it.

123. What is the Lord's Supper?
The eating of bread and the drinking of wine to
remember the sufferings and death of Christ.
(Mark 14:22, 24; 1 Corinthians 11:23–29)

124. What does the bread represent?
The body of Christ, broken for our sins.
(Matthew 26:26; 1 Corinthians 11:24)

125. What does the wine represent?
The blood of Christ, shed for our salvation.
(Matthew 26:27, 28; 1 Corinthians 11:25)

126. Who should partake of the Lord's Supper?
Only those who repent of their sins, believe in
Christ for salvation and love their fellow men.
(Matthew 5:21–24; 1 Corinthians 10:16, 17;
11:18, 20, 27–33; 1 John 3:24–27; 4:9–11)

127. Did Christ remain in the tomb after His
crucifixion?
No. He rose from the tomb on the third day
after His death.
(Luke 24:45–47; 1 Corinthians 15:3, 4)

128. Where is Christ now?
In heaven, seated at the right hand of God
the Father.
(Romans 8:34; Hebrews 1:3; 10:12; 12:2)

129. Will Christ come again?
Yes. At the last day He will come again to
judge the world.
(Matthew 25:31–46; 2 Thessalonians 1:7–10;
2 Timothy 4:1)

130. What happens to men when they die?
The body returns to dust and the soul goes
into the world of spirits.
(Genesis 3:19; Ecclesiastes 12:7; 2 Corinthians
5:1–6)

131. Will the bodies of the dead be raised to life
again?
Yes. "There will be a resurrection of the
dead, both of the just and unjust."
(Daniel 12:2; John 5:28, 29; Acts 24:14, 15)

132. What will happen to the wicked in the day of
judgment?
They shall be cast into hell.
(Psalm 9:16, 17; Luke 12:5; Revelation 20:12–
15)

133. What is hell?
A place of dreadful and endless punishment.
(Matthew 25:46; Mark 9:43–48; Luke 16:19–
31)

134. What will happen to the righteous in the day
of judgment?
They shall live with Christ for ever, in a new
heaven and new earth.
(Isaiah 66:22; 1 Thessalonians 4;16, 17; 2
Peter 3:10–13; Revelation 21:1–4)

135. What is heaven?
A glorious and happy place, where the
righteous shall be forever with the Lord.
(John 14:2, 3; 1 Thessalonians 4:17;
Revelation 21:1–4)

"

The Scriptures of God are my only fountain and
substance in all matters of weight and importance.

"

JOHN OWEN

"

The Bible in memory is better than the Bible
in the book case.

"

C. H. SPURGEON

SCRIPTURE MEMORY

GENESIS 1:1

In the beginning, God created the heavens and the earth.

MATTHEW 22:37

And he said to him, "You shall love the Lord your God with all your heart and with all your soul and with all your mind."

JOHN 3:16

For God so loved the world, that he gave his only Son, that whoever believes in him should not perish but have eternal life.

MATTHEW 22:39

And a second is like it: You shall love your neighbor as yourself.

JOHN 14:6

Jesus said to him, "I am the way, and the truth, and the life. No one comes to the Father except through me."

LUKE 19:10

For the Son of Man came to seek and to save the lost.

EPHESIANS 6:1

Children, obey your parents in the Lord, for this is right.

JOHN 1:1

In the beginning was the Word, and the Word was with God, and the Word was God.

PSALM 122:1

I was glad when they said to me,
"Let us go to the house of the Lord!"

JOHN 4:24

God is spirit, and those who worship him must worship in spirit and truth.

MATTHEW 6:9–13 (THE LORD'S PRAYER)

Pray then like this:
"Our Father in heaven,
hallowed be your name.
Your kingdom come,

your will be done,
on earth as it is in heaven.
Give us this day our daily bread,
and forgive us our debts,
as we also have forgiven our debtors.
And lead us not into temptation,
but deliver us from evil."

PROVERBS 1:8

Hear, my son, your father's instruction,
and forsake not your mother's teaching

JOHN 1:1,14

In the beginning was the Word, and the Word
was with God, and the Word was God. . . . And
the Word became flesh and dwelt among us,
and we have seen his glory, glory as of the
only Son from the Father, full of grace and
truth.

PROVERBS 4:1

Hear, O sons, a father's instruction,
and be attentive, that you may gain insight

PSALM 103:1

Bless the Lord, O my soul,
and all that is within me,
bless his holy name!

ISAIAH 6:3

And one called to another and said:
"Holy, holy, holy is the Lord of hosts;
the whole earth is full of his glory!"

PSALM 145:3

Great is the Lord, and greatly to be praised,
and his greatness is unsearchable.

PSALM 145:8

The Lord is gracious and merciful,
slow to anger and abounding in steadfast love.

PSALM 23

The Lord is my shepherd; I shall not want.
He makes me lie down in green pastures.
He leads me beside still waters.
He restores my soul.
He leads me in paths of righteousness
for his name's sake.

Even though I walk through the valley of the
shadow of death,
I will fear no evil,
for you are with me;
your rod and your staff,
they comfort me.

You prepare a table before me
in the presence of my enemies;
you anoint my head with oil;
my cup overflows.

Surely goodness and mercy shall follow me
all the days of my life,
and I shall dwell in the house of the Lord
forever.

ROMANS 6:23

For the wages of sin is death, but the free gift of
God is eternal life in Christ Jesus our Lord.

JOHN 6:35

Jesus said to them, "I am the bread of life;
whoever comes to me shall not hunger, and
whoever believes in me shall never thirst."

DEUTERONOMY 6:4–5

Hear, O Israel: The Lord our God, the Lord is
one. You shall love the Lord your God with all
your heart and with all your soul and with all
your might.

JOHN 1:29

The next day he saw Jesus coming toward him,
and said, "Behold, the Lamb of God, who takes
away the sin of the world!

PROVERBS 4:1–2

Hear, O sons, a father's instruction,
and be attentive, that you may gain insight,
for I give you good precepts;
do not forsake my teaching.

PROVERBS 1:8–9

Hear, my son, your father's instruction,
and forsake not your mother's teaching,
for they are a graceful garland for your head
and pendants for your neck.

PSALM 145:8–9

The Lord is gracious and merciful,
slow to anger and abounding in steadfast love.
The Lord is good to all,
and his mercy is over all that he has made.

ACTS 16:31

And they said, "Believe in the Lord Jesus, and
you will be saved, you and your household."

LUKE 2:8–15 (THE STORY OF CHRIST'S BIRTH)

And in the same region there were shepherds
out in the field, keeping watch over their flock
by night. And an angel of the Lord appeared to
them, and the glory of the Lord shone around
them, and they were filled with great fear.
And the angel said to them, "Fear not, for
behold, I bring you good news of great joy that
will be for all the people. For unto you is born
this day in the city of David a Savior, who is
Christ the Lord. And this will be a sign for you:
you will find a baby wrapped in swaddling
cloths and lying in a manger." And suddenly
there was with the angel a multitude of the
heavenly host praising God and saying,

"Glory to God in the highest,

and on earth peace among those with whom he is pleased!"

When the angels went away from them into heaven, the shepherds said to one another, "Let us go over to Bethlehem and see this thing that has happened, which the Lord has made known to us."

JOHN 11:25–26

Jesus said to her, "I am the resurrection and the life. Whoever believes in me, though he die, yet shall he live, and everyone who lives and believes in me shall never die. Do you believe this?"

ROMANS 10:9–10

Because, if you confess with your mouth that Jesus is Lord and believe in your heart that God raised him from the dead, you will be saved. For with the heart one believes and is justified, and with the mouth one confesses and is saved.

ROMANS 1:18

For the wrath of God is revealed from heaven against all ungodliness and unrighteousness of men, who by their unrighteousness suppress the truth.

ROMANS 3:23

For the wages of sin is death, but the free gift of
God is eternal life in Christ Jesus our Lord.

PSALM 8

O Lord, our Lord,
how majestic is your name in all the earth!
You have set your glory above the heavens.
Out of the mouth of babies and infants,
you have established strength because of your
foes,
to still the enemy and the avenger.

When I look at your heavens, the work of your
fingers,
the moon and the stars, which you have set in
place,
what is man that you are mindful of him,
and the son of man that you care for him?

Yet you have made him a little lower than the
heavenly beings
and crowned him with glory and honor.
You have given him dominion over the works
of your hands;
you have put all things under his feet,
all sheep and oxen,
and also the beasts of the field,
the birds of the heavens, and the fish of the sea,
whatever passes along the paths of the seas.

O Lord, our Lord,

how majestic is your name in all the earth!

MARK 16:2-8 (THE RESURRECTION OF CHRIST)

And very early on the first day of the week, when the sun had risen, they went to the tomb. And they were saying to one another, "Who will roll away the stone for us from the entrance of the tomb?" And looking up, they saw that the stone had been rolled back—it was very large. And entering the tomb, they saw a young man sitting on the right side, dressed in a white robe, and they were alarmed. And he said to them, "Do not be alarmed. You seek Jesus of Nazareth, who was crucified. He has risen; he is not here. See the place where they laid him. But go, tell his disciples and Peter that he is going before you to Galilee. There you will see him, just as he told you." And they went out and fled from the tomb, for trembling and astonishment had seized them, and they said nothing to anyone, for they were afraid.

PROVERBS 3:5-6

Trust in the Lord with all your heart,
and do not lean on your own understanding.
In all your ways acknowledge him,
and he will make straight your paths.

1 JOHN 3:4

Everyone who makes a practice of sinning also practices lawlessness; sin is lawlessness.

PSALM 100

Make a joyful noise to the Lord, all the earth!
Serve the Lord with gladness!
Come into his presence with singing!

Know that the Lord, he is God!
It is he who made us, and we are his;
we are his people, and the sheep of his pasture.

Enter his gates with thanksgiving,
and his courts with praise!
Give thanks to him; bless his name!

For the Lord is good;
his steadfast love endures forever,
and his faithfulness to all generations.

PROVERBS 20:11

Even a child makes himself known by his acts,
by whether his conduct is pure and upright.

PSALM 119:1–8

Blessed are those whose way is blameless,
who walk in the law of the Lord!
Blessed are those who keep his testimonies,
who seek him with their whole heart,
who also do no wrong,
but walk in his ways!
You have commanded your precepts
to be kept diligently.
Oh that my ways may be steadfast
in keeping your statutes!
Then I shall not be put to shame,
having my eyes fixed on all your commandments.
I will praise you with an upright heart,
when I learn your righteous rules.
I will keep your statutes;
do not utterly forsake me!

JOHN 1:1–4

In the beginning was the Word, and the Word
was with God, and the Word was God. He was
in the beginning with God. All things were
made through him, and without him was not
any thing made that was made. In him was
life, and the life was the light of men.

JOHN 11:25–26

Jesus said to her, "I am the resurrection and the life. Whoever believes in me, though he die, yet shall he live, and everyone who lives and believes in me shall never die. Do you believe this?"

PROVERBS 14:12

There is a way that seems right to a man,
but its end is the way to death.

JOHN 5:24

Truly, truly, I say to you, whoever hears my word and believes him who sent me has eternal life. He does not come into judgment, but has passed from death to life.

PSALM 19

The heavens declare the glory of God,
and the sky above proclaims his handiwork.
Day to day pours out speech,
and night to night reveals knowledge.
There is no speech, nor are there words,
whose voice is not heard.
Their voice goes out through all the earth,
and their words to the end of the world.
In them he has set a tent for the sun,
which comes out like a bridegroom leaving his chamber,
and, like a strong man, runs its course with joy.
Its rising is from the end of the heavens,
and its circuit to the end of them,

and there is nothing hidden from its heat.

The law of the Lord is perfect,
reviving the soul;
the testimony of the Lord is sure,
making wise the simple;
the precepts of the Lord are right,
rejoicing the heart;
the commandment of the Lord is pure,
enlightening the eyes;
the fear of the Lord is clean,
enduring forever;
the rules of the Lord are true,
and righteous altogether.
More to be desired are they than gold,
even much fine gold;
sweeter also than honey
and drippings of the honeycomb.
Moreover, by them is your servant warned;
in keeping them there is great reward.

Who can discern his errors?
Declare me innocent from hidden faults.
Keep back your servant
also from presumptuous sins;
let them not have dominion over me!
Then I shall be blameless,
and innocent of great transgression.

Let the words of my mouth and the meditation
of my heart
be acceptable in your sight,
O Lord, my rock and my redeemer.

JOHN 14:1–6

Let not your hearts be troubled. Believe in God; believe also in me. In my Father's house are many rooms. If it were not so, would I have told you that I go to prepare a place for you? And if I go and prepare a place for you, I will come again and will take you to myself, that where I am you may be also. And you know the way to where I am going." Thomas said to him, "Lord, we do not know where you are going. How can we know the way?" Jesus said to him, "I am the way, and the truth, and the life. No one comes to the Father except through me."

PSALM 119:9–24

Beth

How can a young man keep his way pure?
By guarding it according to your word.
With my whole heart I seek you;
let me not wander from your commandments!
I have stored up your word in my heart,
that I might not sin against you.
Blessed are you, O Lord;
teach me your statutes!
With my lips I declare
all the rules of your mouth.
In the way of your testimonies I delight
as much as in all riches.
I will meditate on your precepts
and fix my eyes on your ways.
I will delight in your statutes;
I will not forget your word.

Gimel
Deal bountifully with your servant,
that I may live and keep your word.
Open my eyes, that I may behold
wondrous things out of your law.
I am a sojourner on the earth;
hide not your commandments from me!
My soul is consumed with longing
for your rules at all times.
You rebuke the insolent, accursed ones,
who wander from your commandments.
Take away from me scorn and contempt,
for I have kept your testimonies.
Even though princes sit plotting against me,
your servant will meditate on your statutes.
Your testimonies are my delight;
they are my counselors.

PROVERBS 12:26

One who is righteous is a guide to his neighbor,
but the way of the wicked leads them astray.

1 JOHN 5:4–5

For everyone who has been born of God
overcomes the world. And this is the victory
that has overcome the world—our faith. Who is
it that overcomes the world except the one
who believes that Jesus is the Son of God?

MATTHEW 6:19–21

Do not lay up for yourselves treasures on earth, where moth and rust destroy and where thieves break in and steal, but lay up for yourselves treasures in heaven, where neither moth nor rust destroys and where thieves do not break in and steal. For where your treasure is, there your heart will be also.

MATTHEW 6:24–26

No one can serve two masters, for either he will hate the one and love the other, or he will be devoted to the one and despise the other. You cannot serve God and money.

"Therefore I tell you, do not be anxious about your life, what you will eat or what you will drink, nor about your body, what you will put on. Is not life more than food, and the body more than clothing? Look at the birds of the air: they neither sow nor reap nor gather into barns, and yet your heavenly Father feeds them. Are you not of more value than they?

MATTHEW 5:1–12 (THE BEATITUDES)

Seeing the crowds, he went up on the mountain, and when he sat down, his disciples came to him.

And he opened his mouth and taught them, saying:

"Blessed are the poor in spirit, for theirs is the kingdom of heaven.

"Blessed are those who mourn, for they shall be comforted.

"Blessed are the meek, for they shall inherit the earth.

"Blessed are those who hunger and thirst for righteousness, for they shall be satisfied.

"Blessed are the merciful, for they shall receive mercy.

"Blessed are the pure in heart, for they shall see God.

"Blessed are the peacemakers, for they shall be called sons of God.

"Blessed are those who are persecuted for righteousness' sake, for theirs is the kingdom of heaven.

"Blessed are you when others revile you and persecute you and utter all kinds of evil against you falsely on my account. Rejoice and be glad, for your reward is great in heaven, for so they persecuted the prophets who were before you."

PSALM 119:25-40

Daleth
My soul clings to the dust;
give me life according to your word!
When I told of my ways, you answered me;
teach me your statutes!
Make me understand the way of your precepts,
and I will meditate on your wondrous works.
My soul melts away for sorrow;

strengthen me according to your word!
Put false ways far from me
and graciously teach me your law!
I have chosen the way of faithfulness;
I set your rules before me.
I cling to your testimonies, O Lord;
let me not be put to shame!
I will run in the way of your commandments
when you enlarge my heart!

He
Teach me, O Lord, the way of your statutes;
and I will keep it to the end.
Give me understanding, that I may keep
your law
and observe it with my whole heart.
Lead me in the path of your commandments,
for I delight in it.
Incline my heart to your testimonies,
and not to selfish gain!
Turn my eyes from looking at worthless
things;
and give me life in your ways.
Confirm to your servant your promise,
that you may be feared.
Turn away the reproach that I dread,
for your rules are good.
Behold, I long for your precepts;
in your righteousness give me life!

JOHN 10:9–10

I am the door. If anyone enters by me, he will be saved and will go in and out and find pasture. The thief comes only to steal and kill and destroy. I came that they may have life and have it abundantly.

"

Always stand to it that your creed must bend
to the Bible, and not the Bible to your creed.

"

C. H. SPURGEON

"

Children are not a distraction from more important
work, they are the most important work.

"

C. S. LEWIS

BIBLE BASICS

THE TEN COMMANDMENTS
Summarized Version

1. You shall have no other gods before me.
2. You shall not make for yourself any carved image.
3. You shall not take the name of the LORD your God in vain.
4. Remember the Sabbath day, to keep it holy.
5. Honor your father and mother.
6. You shall not murder.
7. You shall not commit adultery.
8. You shall not steal.
9. You shall not bear false witness.
10. You shall not covet.

THE LORD'S PRAYER
Matthew 6:9-13

Pray then like this:
"Our Father in heaven,
hallowed be your name.
Your kingdom come,
your will be done,
on earth as it is in heaven.
Give us this day our daily bread,
and forgive us our debts,
as we also have forgiven our debtors.
And lead us not into temptation,
but deliver us from evil.

NAMES OF THE TWELVE APOSTLES

1. Simon Peter
2. Andrew
3. James (son of Zebedee)
4. John (son of Zebedee)
5. Philip
6. Bartholomew
7. Matthew
8. Thomas
9. James (son of Alphaeus)
10. Simon
11. Thaddaeus (Judas, son of James)
12. Judas Iscariot

THE APOSTLES' CREED

I believe in God, the Father Almighty,
the Maker of heaven and earth,
and in Jesus Christ, His only Son, our Lord:
Who was conceived by the Holy Ghost,
born of the virgin Mary,
suffered under Pontius Pilate,
was crucified, dead, and buried;
He descended into hell.
The third day He arose again from the dead;
He ascended into heaven,
and sitteth on the right hand of God the Father
Almighty;
from thence he shall come to judge the quick and
the dead.
I believe in the Holy Ghost;
the holy catholic church;
the communion of saints;
the forgiveness of sins;
the resurrection of the body;
and the life everlasting.
Amen.

(NOTE: The meaning of "catholic" is not to be confused with the Roman Catholic Church. It means universal.)

THE BOOKS OF THE BIBLE

Old Testament		
Genesis	II Chronicles	Daniel
Exodus	Ezra	Hosea
Leviticus	Nehemiah	Joel
Numbers	Esther	Amos
Deuteronomy	Job	Obadiah
Joshua	Psalm	Jonah
Judges	Proverbs	Micah
Ruth	Ecclesiastes	Nahum
I Samuel	Song of Solomon	Habakkuk
II Samuel	Isaiah	Zephaniah
I Kings	Jeremiah	Haggai
II Kings	Lamentations	Zechariah
I Chronicles	Ezekiel	Malachi

New Testament		
Matthew	Ephesians	Hebrews
Mark	Philippians	James
Luke	Colossians	I Peter
John	I Thessalonians	II Peter
Acts	II Thessalonians	I John
Romans	I Timothy	II John
I Corinthians	II Timothy	III John
II Corinthians	Titus	Jude
Galatians	Philemon	Revelation

THE NICENE CREED

I believe in one God, the Father Almighty, Maker of heaven and earth, and of all things visible and invisible.

And in one Lord Jesus Christ, the only-begotten Son of God, begotten of the Father before all worlds; God of God, Light of Light, very God of very God; begotten, not made, being of one substance with the Father, by whom all things were made.

Who, for us men and for our salvation, came down from heaven, and was incarnate by the Holy Spirit of the virgin Mary, and was made man; and was crucified also for us under Pontius Pilate; He suffered and was buried; and the third day He rose again, according to the Scriptures; and ascended into heaven, and sits on the right hand of the Father; and He shall come again, with glory, to judge the quick and the dead; whose kingdom shall have no end.

And I believe in the Holy Ghost, the Lord and Giver of Life; who proceeds from the Father and the Son; who with the Father and the Son together is worshipped and glorified; who spoke by the prophets.

And I believe in one holy catholic and apostolic Church. I acknowledge one baptism for the remission of sins; and I look for the resurrection of the dead, and the life of the world to come. Amen.

"

Beautiful music is the art of the prophets that can calm the agitations of the soul; it is one of the most magnificent and delightful presents God has given us.

"

MARTIN LUTHER

"

The foundation of worship in the heart is not emotional it is theological.

"

SINCLAIR FERGUSON

HYMNS

DOXOLOGY

Words by Thomas Ken (1674)

Praise God, from Whom all blessings flow;
Praise Him, all creatures here below;
Praise Him above, ye heavenly host;
Praise Father, Son, and Holy Ghost.

Amen.

JESUS LOVES ME
Words by Anna Bartlett Warner (1860)

Verse 1

Jesus loves me! this I know,
For the Bible tells me so;
Little ones to Him belong;
They are weak, but He is strong.

Refrain

Yes, Jesus loves me!
Yes, Jesus loves me!
Yes, Jesus loves me!
The Bible tells me so.

Verse 2

Jesus loves me he who died
heaven's gate to open wide.
He will wash away my sin,
let his little child come in.

Refrain

Verse 3

Jesus loves me, this I know,
as he loved so long ago,
taking children on his knee,
saying, "Let them come to me.

Refrain

HOLY, HOLY, HOLY
Words by Reginald Heber (1826)

Verse 1

Holy, holy, holy! Lord God Almighty!
Early in the morning our song shall rise to Thee;
Holy, holy, holy, merciful and mighty!
God in three Persons, blessèd Trinity!

Verse 2

Holy, holy, holy! all the saints adore Thee,
Casting down their golden crowns around the glassy sea;
Cherubim and seraphim falling down before Thee,
Who wert, and art, and evermore shall be.

Verse 3

Holy, holy, holy! tho' the darkness hide Thee,
Tho' the eye of sinful man Thy glory may not see;
Only Thou art holy; there is none beside Thee,
Perfect in power, in love, and purity.

Verse 4

Holy, holy, holy! Lord God Almighty!
All Thy works shall praise
Thy Name, in earth, and sky, and sea;
Holy, holy, holy; merciful and mighty!
God in three Persons, blessed Trinity!

BLESS THE LORD OH MY SOUL
Words by Matt Redman (2001)

Verse 1

The sun comes up
It's a new day dawning
It's time to sing Your song again
Whatever may pass
And whatever lies before me
Let me be singing
When the evening comes

Refrain

Bless the Lord oh my soul
Oh my soul
Worship His Holy name
Sing like never before
Oh my soul
I'll worship Your Holy name

Verse 2

You're rich in love
And You're slow to anger
Your name is great
And Your heart is kind
For all Your goodness
I will keep on singing
Ten thousand reasons
For my heart to find

Refrain

Verse 3

And on that day
When my strength is failing
The end draws near
And my time has come
Still my soul will
Sing Your praise unending
Ten thousand years
And then forevermore

Refrain

REJOICE, THE LORD IS KING
Words by Charles Wesley (1744)

Verse 1

Rejoice, the Lord is King!
Your Lord and King adore!
Rejoice, give thanks and sing,
And triumph evermore:
Lift up your heart, lift up your voice!
Rejoice, again I say, rejoice!

Verse 2

Jesus, the Savior, reigns,
The God of truth and love;
When He had purged our stains,
He took His seat above;
Lift up your heart, lift up your voice!
Rejoice, again I say, rejoice!

Verse 3

His kingdom cannot fail,
He rules o'er earth and heav'n;
The keys of death and hell
Are to our Jesus given;
Lift up your heart, lift up your voice!
Rejoice, again I say, rejoice!

Verse 3

Rejoice in glorious hope!
Our Lord and judge shall come
And take His servants up
To their eternal home:
Lift up your heart,
Lift up your voice!
Rejoice, again I say, rejoice!

Amen.

FAIREST LORD JESUS
Words by an Anonymous German
Author (17th-Century)

Verse 1

Fairest Lord Jesus, Ruler of all nature,
O Thou of God and man the Son;
Thee will I cherish, Thee will I honor,
Thou, my soul's glory, joy and crown.

Verse 2

Fair are the meadows, Fairer still the woodlands,
Robed in the blooming garb of spring;
Jesus is fairer, Jesus is purer,
Who makes the woeful heart to sing.

Verse 3

Fair is the sunshine, Fairer still the moonlight,
And all the twinkling, starry host;
Jesus shines brighter, Jesus shines purer
Than all the angels heaven can boast.

Amen.

THIS IS MY FATHER'S WORLD
Words by Maltbie D. Babcock (1901)

Verse 1

This is my Father's world,
And to my listening ears,
All nature sings,
And round me rings
The music of the spheres.
This is my Father's world,
I rest me in the thought
Of rocks and trees, of skies and seas;
His hand the wonders wrought.

Verse 2

This is my Father's world,
The birds their carols raise;
The morning light, the lily white
Declare their Maker's praise.
This is my Father's world:
He shines in all that's fair;
In the rustling grass I hear Him pass,
He speaks to me everywhere.

Verse 3

This is my Father's world,
O let me ne'er forget
That though the wrong seems oft so strong,
God is the ruler yet.
This is my Father's world,
The battle is not done;
Jesus who died shall be satisfied,
And earth and heaven be one.

Amen.

HE WILL HOLD ME FAST
Words by Ada R. Habershon (1906)

Verse1

"When I fear my faith will fail
Christ will hold me fast
When the tempter would prevail
He will hold me fast
I could never keep my hold
Through life's fearful path
For my love is often cold
He must hold me fast

Refrain

He will hold me fast
He will hold me fast
For my Savior loves me so
He will hold me fast

Verse 2

Those He saves are His delight
Christ will hold me fast
Precious in His holy sight
He will hold me fast
He'll not let my soul be lost
His promises shall last
Bought by Him at such a cost
He will hold me fast

Refrain

Verse 3

For my life He bled and died
Christ will hold me fast
Justice has been satisfied
He will hold me fast

Raised with Him to endless life
He will hold me fast
Till our faith is turned to sight
When he comes at last

Refrain

ROCK OF AGES, CLEFT FOR ME
Words by Augustus Toplady (1776)

Verse 1

Rock of Ages, cleft for me,
let me hide myself in thee;
let the water and the blood,
from thy wounded side which flowed,
be of sin the double cure;
save from wrath and make me pure.

Verse 2

Not the labors of my hands
can fulfill thy law's commands;
could my zeal no respite know,
could my tears forever flow,
all for sin could not atone;
thou must save, and thou alone.

Verse 3

Nothing in my hand I bring,
simply to the cross I cling;
naked, come to thee for dress;
helpless, look to thee for grace;
foul, I to the fountain fly;
wash me, Savior, or I die.

Verse 4

While I draw this fleeting breath,
when mine eyes shall close in death,
when I soar to worlds unknown,
see thee on thy judgment throne,
Rock of Ages, cleft for me,
let me hide myself in thee.

"

The word of God can be in the mind without being in the heart, but it cannot be in the heart without first being in the mind.

"

R. C. SPROUL

"

You may speak but a word to a child, and in that child there may be slumbering a noble heart which shall stir the Christian Church in years to come.

"

C. H. SPURGEON

TRACK YOUR PROGRESS

The following is a suggested guide of memory work from Book 1 divided into suggested ages with a column to record the date of mastery. If you are not beginning age two and three, we suggest that you begin with the recommended scripture, hymns, etc. for your child by age, as well as with question #1 of *A Catechism for Boys and Girls*. The catechism is written in a systematic format with each question built upon those before it. The memorization of the whole catechism will expose the child to a solid doctrinal foundation.

AGES TWO AND THREE
A Catechism for Boys and Girls

Question #1-5   Date: _____

Scripture Memory

Genesis 1:1   Date: _____
Matthew 22:37   Date: _____
John 3:16   Date: _____
Matthew 22:39   Date: _____
John 14:6   Date: _____
Luke 19:10   Date: _____
Ephesians 6:1   Date: _____
John 1:1   Date: _____

Hymns

Doxology   Date: _____
Jesus Loves Me   Date: _____

AGE FOUR

A Catechism for Boys and Girls

Question #6-10   Date: _____
Question #11-15   Date: _____

Scripture Memory

Psalm 122:1   Date: _____
John 4:24   Date: _____
Matthew 6:9–13   Date: _____
Proverbs 1:8   Date: _____
John 1:1,14   Date: _____
Proverbs 4:1-2   Date: _____
Psalm 103:1   Date: _____
Isaiah 6:3   Date: _____
Psalm 145:3   Date: _____
Psalm 145:8   Date: _____

Hymns

Holy, Holy, Holy   Date: _____

AGE FIVE

A Catechism for Boys and Girls

Question #16-20   Date: _____
Question #21-24   Date: _____

Scripture Memory

Psalm 23   Date: _____
Romans 6:23   Date: _____
John 6:35   Date: _____
Deuteronomy 6:4–5   Date: _____
John 1:29   Date: _____
Proverbs 4:1   Date: _____
Proverbs 1:8–9   Date: _____
Psalm 145:8–9   Date: _____
Acts 16:31   Date: _____

Hymns

Bless the Lord Oh My Soul   Date: _____
Rejoice, the Lord is King   Date: _____
Holy, Holy, Holy   Date: _____

AGE SIX

A Catechism for Boys and Girls

Question #25-30   Date: _____
Question #31-35   Date: _____
Question #36-40   Date: _____
Question #41-45   Date: _____

Scripture Memory

Luke 2:8–15   Date: _____
John 11:25–26   Date: _____
Romans 10:9–10   Date: _____
Romans 1:18   Date: _____
Romans 3:23   Date: _____
Psalm 8   Date: _____

Bible Basics

The Ten Commandments   Date: _____
The Lord's Prayer   Date: _____

Hymns

Fairest Lord Jesus   Date: _____
Rejoice, the Lord is King   Date: _____

AGE SEVEN

A Catechism for Boys and Girls

Question #46-50   Date: _____

Question #51-55   Date: _____

Question #56-60   Date: _____

Question #61-65   Date: _____

Question #66-71   Date: _____

Scripture Memory

Mark 16:2–8   Date: _____

Proverbs 3:5–6   Date: _____

1 John 3:4   Date: _____

Psalm 100   Date: _____

Proverbs 20:11   Date: _____

Psalm 119:1–8   Date: _____

Bible Basics

The Names of
the Twelve Apostles   Date: _____

The Apostles' Creed   Date: _____

Hymns

This is My Father's World   Date: _____

AGE EIGHT

A Catechism for Boys and Girls

Question #72-77   Date: _____
Question #78-83   Date: _____
Question #84-89   Date: _____
Question #90-96   Date: _____

Scripture Memory

John 1:1–4   Date: _____
John 11:25–26   Date: _____
Proverbs 14:12   Date: _____
John 5:24   Date: _____
Psalm 19   Date: _____
John 14:1–6   Date: _____
Psalm 119:9–24   Date: _____
Proverbs 12:26   Date: _____

Bible Basics

The Books of the Bible   Date: _____

Hymns

He Will Hold Me Fast   Date: _____

AGE NINE

A Catechism for Boys and Girls

Question #97-102   Date: _____
Question #103-108   Date: _____
Question #109-114   Date: _____
Question #115-119   Date: _____
Question #120-124   Date: _____
Question #125-129   Date: _____
Question #130-135   Date: _____

Scripture Memory

1 John 5:4–5   Date: _____
Matthew 6:19–21   Date: _____
Matthew 6:24–26   Date: _____
Matthew 5:1–12   Date: _____
Psalm 119:25–40   Date: _____
John 10:9–10   Date: _____

Bible Basics

The Nicene Creed   Date: _____

Hymns

Rock of Ages, Cleft for Me   Date: _____